MANNERS *of the* HEART
STUDENT WORKBOOK

Student Activity Sheets & Home Connection Letters

KINDERGARTEN

This book belongs to:

_____

Published by **MANNERS** of the **HEART**

763 North Boulevard
Baton Rouge, LA 70802
225.383.3235
www.mannersoftheheart.org

Third Edition
Copyright 2020 by **MANNERS** of the **HEART**
All rights reserved.
Printed in the United States of America.

Author: Jill Rigby Garner
Editor: Angelle High
Editor at large: Angelle Roddy
Graphic Design: Shelby Bailey, Loren Barilleau
Cover Design: Brian Rivet
Merryville Stories: Nick and Jill Garner, Micah Webber, Janie Spaht Gill, Ph.D.
Contributor: Emily Jones
Photography: Darlene Aguillard, McCauley Mills, Taylor Frey

MANNERS of the **HEART** grants teachers the right to photocopy the reproducibles from this book for classroom use. No other part of this publication may be reproduced, stored in a retrieval system, or transmitted in any form or by any means—electronic, mechanical, photocopy, recording, or any other, without the prior written permission of the publisher. Please direct all questions and inquiries to:

info@mannersoftheheart.org or
MANNERS of the **HEART**
763 North Boulevard
Baton Rouge, LA 70802
www.mannersoftheheart.org

STUDENT ACTIVITY SHEETS

Student Activity Sheet - Week 1

Manners in Merryville

Draw the Happle Tree!

Name

Student Activity Sheet - Week 1

Map of Merryville

Student Activity Sheet - Week 2

Wise Ol' Wilbur

Draw and color a portrait of Wilbur!

Name

Student Activity Sheet - Week 3

Stop for Respect

Color the symbols below. What does each one stand for?

Name

Student Activity Sheet - Week 4

Duty Chart

List each of your duties at home. Check or color the box when you complete a duty on that day.

Duties:	Sunday	Monday	Tuesday	Wednesday	Thursday	Friday	Saturday

Name _____

Student Activity Sheet - Week 5

Flower Pot

What will the seeds become? Draw and color your own flowers!

Name

Student Activity Sheet - Week 6

Name

Student Activity Sheet - Week 6

Name

Student Activity Sheet - Week 7

Being a Bully

What does bullying look like? Draw a scene where someone is being bullied.

_____
Name

Student Activity Sheet - Week 8

The Happle Tree Treetop

Student Activity Sheet - Week 8

The Happle Tree

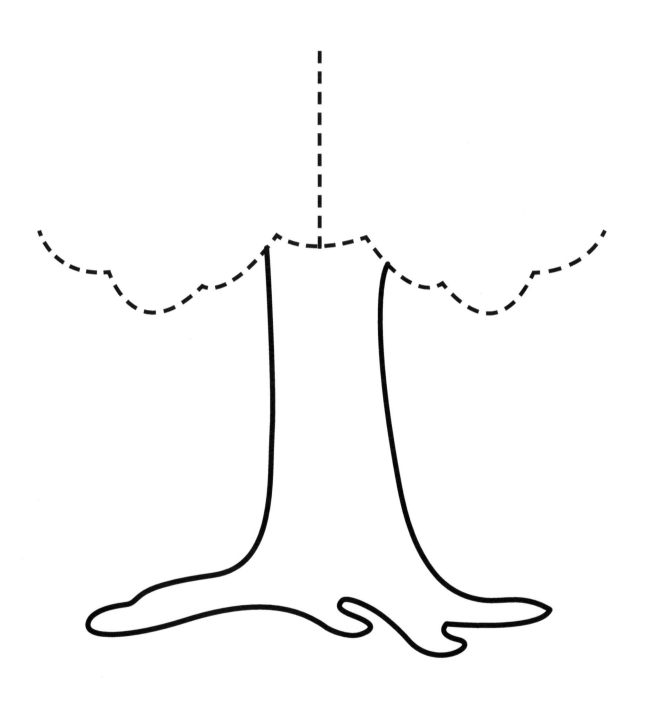

Name

Student Activity Sheet - Week 8

Wilbur Says

_____
Name

Student Activity Sheet - Week 11

Being a Guest

Use your imagination! In whose home would you like to be a guest?

_____
Name

Student Activity Sheet - Week 12

"Hello, World"

Color our world and the children who make it special.

_____
Name

Student Activity Sheet - Week 13

LEARN

Put the first letter of the sentence in each block and LEARN how to spell a new word!

- [ ] ook in the eyes
- [ ] nd talking and moving
- [ ] nswer questions when asked
- [ ] emain quiet (no interruptions!)
- [ ] od your head

___ ___ ___ ___ ___

Name

Student Activity Sheet - Week 14

Chatterbox

Color and cut out the phone. Glue your phone onto an index card.

Student Activity Sheet - Week 15

Thank You Card

Cut out the card and fold it in half. Draw a picture on the front.
On the inside, write Thank You! Love, (your name).

Student Activity Sheet - Week 17

Wilbur's Kindness Pledge

Today I pledge to wait my turn.
Put others first, so I can learn.
Today I pledge to help my friends.
It's how you play and not who wins!

_____
Name

_____
Date

Student Activity Sheet - Week 18

Let the Circle Be Unbroken

Color and then cut out the puzzle!

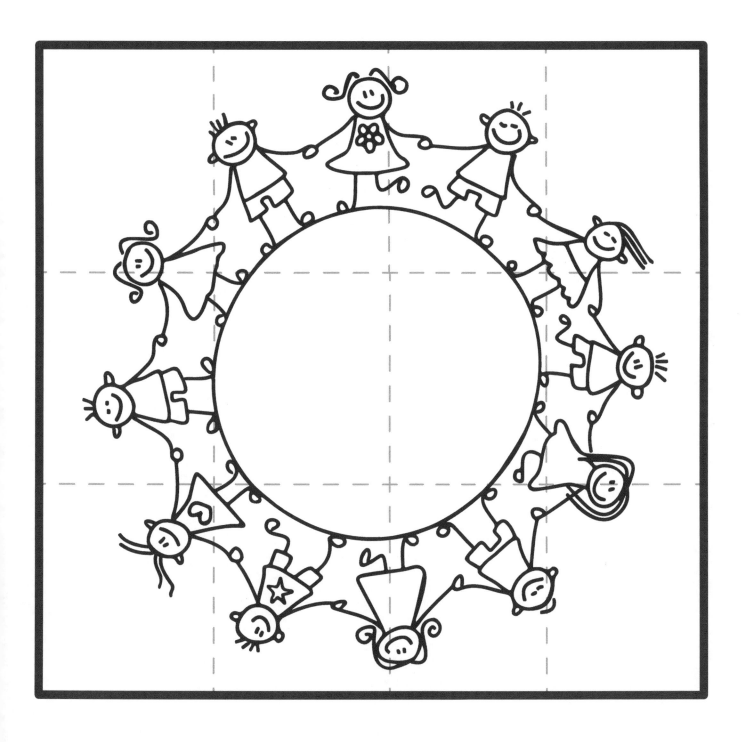

Student Activity Sheet - Week 19

Door Hanger

Student Activity Sheet - Week 20

If You...

If you open it, close it.

If you turn it on, turn it off.

If you unlock it, lock it.

If you spill it, clean it up.

If you take it out, put it back.

If you break it, fix it.

Cap'n Nick

Name

Student Activity Sheet - Week 21

Just Act Respectfully

If you see someone drop something, you should… *Help them pick it up!*	If a friend gives you a present and you already have one, you should say… *Thank you! (This looks like fun!)*
If you are eating with others and you finish your meal first, you should… *Sit quietly and enjoy the conversation!*	If you don't like the food being served, you should… *Still eat a "courtesy bite" or say, "No, thank you" with a smile!*
When a guest is leaving, you should say… *Thank you very much for coming! I had fun!*	Show me the kind of voice you should use if you are at a gathering with friends or family… *Your inside voice! (No yelling!)*
While at the dinner table, don't talk with your mouth… *Full! (Close your mouth to chew and then you can talk!)*	If someone has her arms full and is trying to open the door, you should… *Open the door for her!*
If you accidentally spill something, you should… *Clean it up!*	You greet a guest at your party by saying… *Hello! Thank you for coming!*
When there is a crowd of people you need to get through, you do not shove, but instead say… *Please excuse me!*	If you are at a birthday party and you are invited to play in a game, you should… *Play!*
When you leave someone's home, you should say… *Thank you for having me! I had fun!*	If there is a long line, you should… *Wait nicely for your turn! (Don't complain!)*
When an elderly person is looking for a seat, you should… *Offer him/her your seat!*	How do you put food on your plate at a party? *With a serving utensil or touching only the one you are taking!*

Student Activity Sheet - Week 22

Old Glory

Name

Student Activity Sheet - Week 22

Our Flag

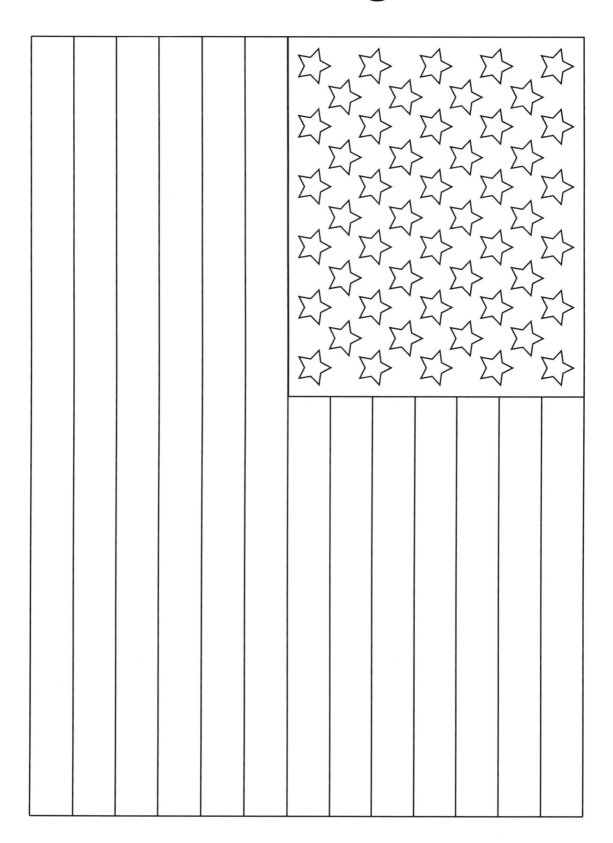

Name

GLOSSARY

WILBUR'S GLOSSARY

A

ACCEPTANCE
Treating everyone I meet with respect, even when they are different from me

APPRECIATION
Recognizing value in people, places and things

APPROPRIATE
Knowing the right thing to say or do

C

CITIZENSHIP
An attitude of cooperation for the good of everyone

CIVIL
Respecting others and myself for the good of our community

CONSCIENTIOUS
Diligently careful

CONSIDERATE
Thinking about the feelings of others before I speak or act

COOPERATION
Choosing to be helpful, not hurtful, when I work with others

COURTESY
Respectful and well-mannered words and actions toward others

E

EMPATHY
Walking in another person's shoes

ENCOURAGEMENT
Offering words to others to build their confidence

EXPRESSIVE
Showing what is in my heart

WILBUR'S GLOSSARY

F

FORGIVENESS
Choosing to let go of bad feelings toward another person

FRIENDLINESS
Welcoming others by offering a quick smile and a kind word

G

GENEROSITY
Gladly giving my time, talent and treasure

GENTLE
Speaking and acting with tenderness

GOODNESS
Being kind and forgiving

GRACIOUS
Being polite, understanding and generous in all situations

GRATEFUL
Giving thanks from the heart

H

HONOR
Showing respect to others because of who they are

HOSPITALITY
Serving others so they feel cared for and comfortable

HUMBLE CONFIDENCE
The courage to be my best so that I can help others become their best

HUMILITY
Not caring who gets credit

K

KINDNESS
Showing care for others in an unexpected and exceptional way

WILBUR'S GLOSSARY

L

LOVE
Genuinely caring for others

LOYALTY
Faithful devotion

M

MANNERS
An attitude of the heart that puts the needs of others ahead of my own

MATURITY
Making the right choice, even when others around me do not

O

OBEDIENCE
Choosing to do what I am told to do

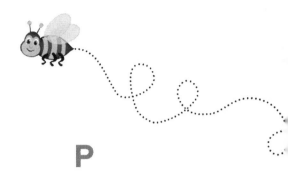

P

PARTICIPATION
Jumping in to do my part

PATIENCE
Choosing to wait without complaining

PATRIOTISM
Loving my country

POLITE
Using kind words and actions

R

RESOURCEFUL
Using my imagination to fix everyday problems

WILBUR'S GLOSSARY

RESPECT
Treating others with dignity

RESPONSIBILITY
Following through on my work without being reminded

S

SELF-CONTROL
Managing myself when no one is looking

SELF-ESTEEM
Self-absorption, presenting itself as self-conceit on one extreme and self-consciousness on the other

SELF-RESPECT
A character trait that results from treating others with dignity

SELFLESS
Giving to others without thinking of myself

SPORTSMANSHIP
Being more concerned with helping my team than helping myself

T

THOUGHTFUL
Looking for ways to make others feel loved

TRUSTWORTHY
Doing what you said you would do when you said you would do it

U

UNDERSTANDING
Accepting others for who they are

The Education of the HEART must be the HEART of Education

 763 North Boulevard,
Baton Rouge, LA 70802

 www.mannersoftheheart.org

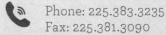 Phone: 225.383.3235
Fax: 225.381.3090

Made in the USA
Columbia, SC
15 May 2024